S0-BXH-147

Love Bears All Things

# Warm
# Fuzzies

## For Your
## Heart

*Zondervan Gifts*

A happy heart makes
the face cheerful.

Proverbs 15:13

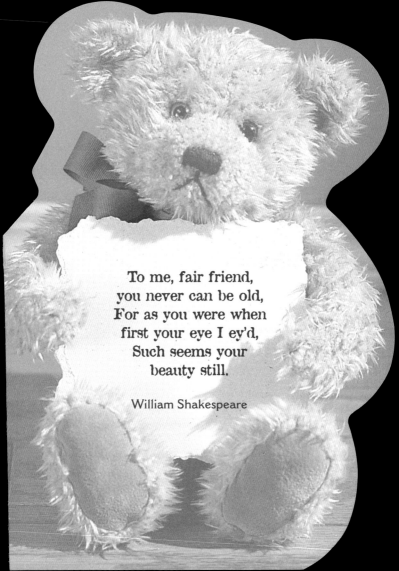

To me, fair friend,
you never can be old,
For as you were when
first your eye I ey'd,
Such seems your
beauty still.

William Shakespeare

A true friend will see you through when others see that you are through.

Unknown

Carry each other's
burdens, and in this
way you will fulfill the
law of Christ.

Galatians 6:2

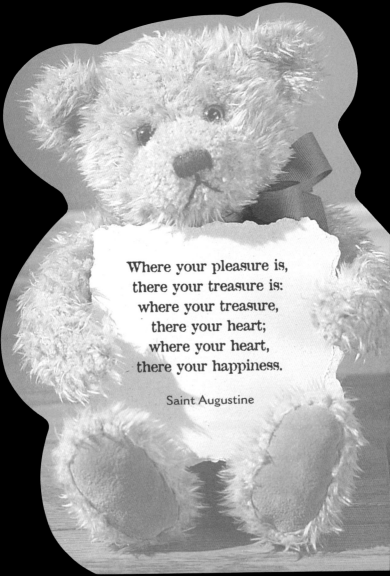

Where your pleasure is,
there your treasure is:
where your treasure,
there your heart;
where your heart,
there your happiness.

**Saint Augustine**

Commit your way to
the LORD; trust in him
and he will do this:
He will make your
righteousness shine
like the dawn,
the justice of your
cause like the
noonday sun.

Psalm 37:5 –6

The LORD gives strength
to his people;
the LORD blesses his
people with peace.

Psalm 29:11

The happiest heart
that ever beat
Was in some quiet breast
That found the common
daylight sweet,
And left to Heaven
the rest.

John Vance Cheney

How soon a smile of
God can change the
world!

Robert Browning

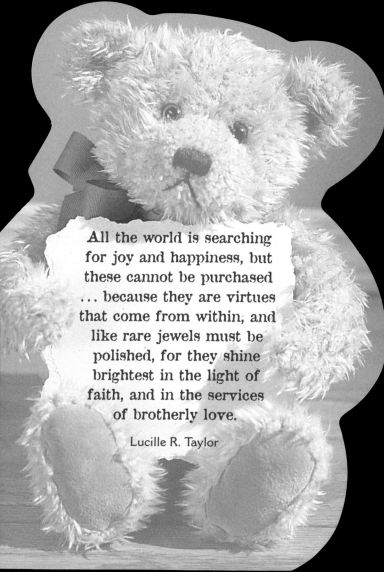

All the world is searching
for joy and happiness, but
these cannot be purchased
... because they are virtues
that come from within, and
like rare jewels must be
polished, for they shine
brightest in the light of
faith, and in the services
of brotherly love.

Lucille R. Taylor

The fruit of the Spirit is
love, joy, peace, patience,
kindness, goodness, faith-
fulness, gentleness and
self-control.

Galatians 5:22 –23

The kiss of the sun
for pardon,
The song of the birds
for mirth,
One is nearer God's heart
in a garden
Than anywhere else
on earth.

Dorothy Frances Gurney

Kind words are the music of the world. They have a power which seems to be beyond natural causes, as if they were some angel's song which had lost its way and come on earth.

Frederick William Faber

Love is the doorway
though which the human
soul passes from selfish-
ness to service and from
solitude to kinship with
mankind.

Anonymous

Friendship consists in forgetting what one gives and remembering what one receives.

Alexandre Dumas

Many flowers open to the sun, but only one follows him constantly. Heart, be thou the sunflower, not only open to receive God's blessing, but constant in looking to him.

Jean Paul Richter

May the God of hope fill
you with all joy and peace
as you trust in him, so
that you may overflow
with hope by the power
of the Holy Spirit.

Romans 15:13

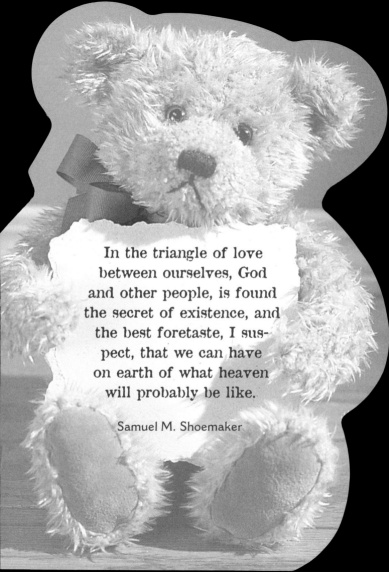

In the triangle of love
between ourselves, God
and other people, is found
the secret of existence, and
the best foretaste, I sus-
pect, that we can have
on earth of what heaven
will probably be like.

Samuel M. Shoemaker

Love makes all hard
hearts gentle.

George Herbert

Eternity is the divine treasure house, and hope is the
window, by means of which
mortals are permitted to
see, as through a glass
darkly, the things which
God is preparing.

William Mountford

You understand, O LORD;
remember me and care
for me.

Jeremiah 15:15

Love isn't a reservoir.
You'll never drain it dry.
It's much more like a natural spring. The longer and
the farther it flows, the
stronger and the deeper
and the clearer it becomes.

Eddie Cantor

Sing to the LORD
a new song;
sing to the LORD,
all the earth.

Psalm 96:1

Divine love is a sacred
flower, which in its early
bud is happiness, and in its
full bloom is heaven.

Eleanor Louisa Hervey

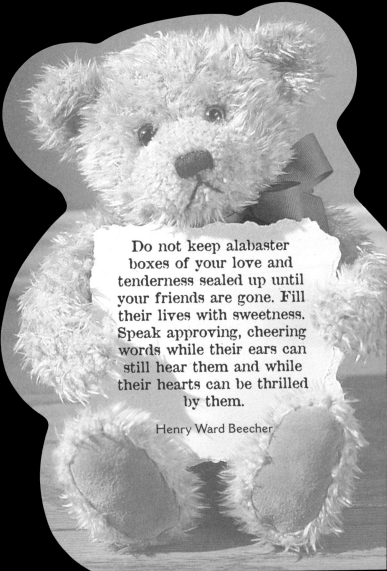

Do not keep alabaster boxes of your love and tenderness sealed up until your friends are gone. Fill their lives with sweetness. Speak approving, cheering words while their ears can still hear them and while their hearts can be thrilled by them.

Henry Ward Beecher

Build bridges instead
of walls and you will have
a friend.

Unknown

Come, let us bow down in worship, let us kneel before the LORD our Maker; for he is our God and we are the people of his pasture, the flock under his care.

Psalm 95:6–7

Friends are those rare
people who ask how we
are and then wait to hear
the answer.

Ed Cunningham

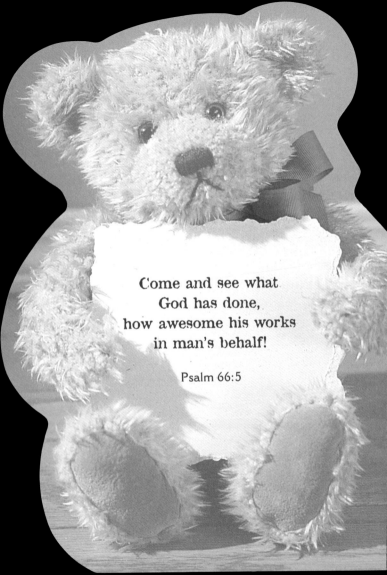

Come and see what
God has done,
how awesome his works
in man's behalf!

Psalm 66:5

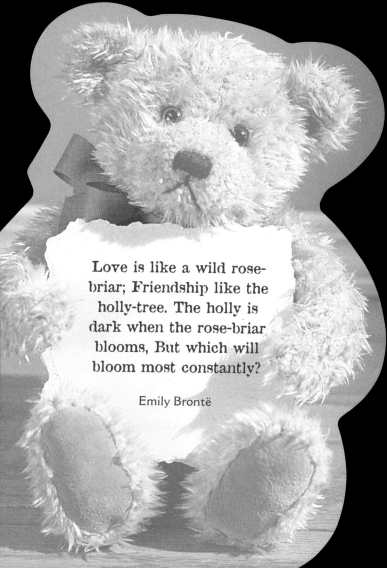

Love is like a wild rose-briar; Friendship like the holly-tree. The holly is dark when the rose-briar blooms, But which will bloom most constantly?

Emily Brontë

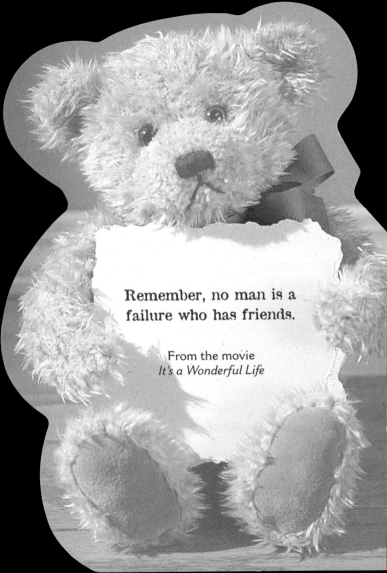

Remember, no man is a
failure who has friends.

From the movie
*It's a Wonderful Life*

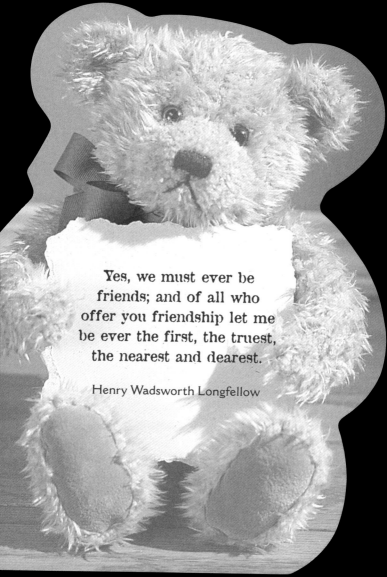

Yes, we must ever be
friends; and of all who
offer you friendship let me
be ever the first, the truest,
the nearest and dearest.

Henry Wadsworth Longfellow

The heart benevolent
and kind the most
resembles God.

Robert Burns

The LORD will be the sure
foundation for your times,
a rich store of salvation and
wisdom and knowledge; the
fear of the LORD is the
key to this treasure.

Isaiah 33:6

Mercy, peace and love be
yours in abundance.

Jude 2

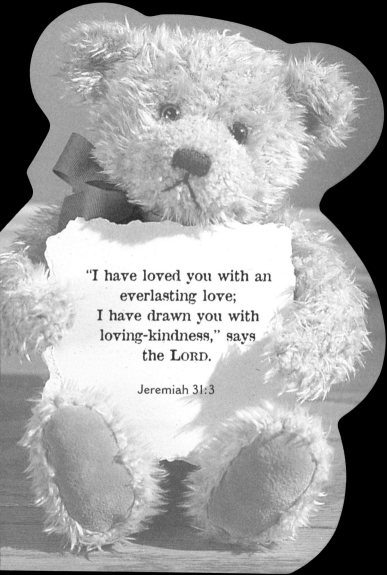

"I have loved you with an everlasting love;
I have drawn you with loving-kindness," says
the LORD.

Jeremiah 31:3

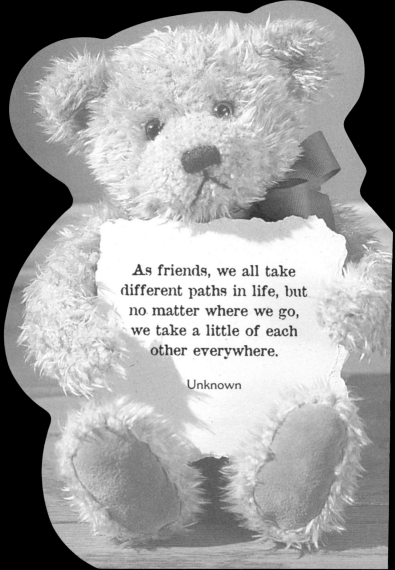

As friends, we all take
different paths in life, but
no matter where we go,
we take a little of each
other everywhere.

Unknown

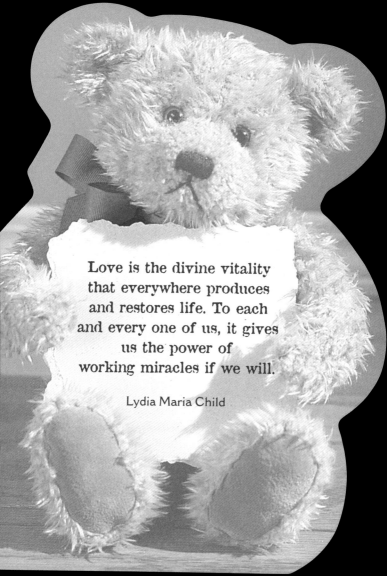

Love is the divine vitality
that everywhere produces
and restores life. To each
and every one of us, it gives
us the power of
working miracles if we will.

Lydia Maria Child

How fit to employ
All the heart and the
soul and the senses
forever in joy!

Robert Browning

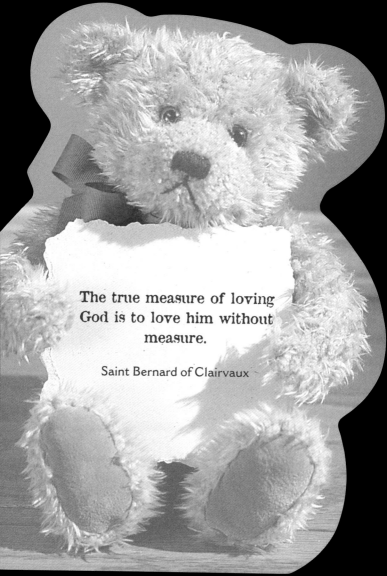

The true measure of loving God is to love him without measure.

Saint Bernard of Clairvaux

Our lives are songs; God
writes the words
And we set them to
music at pleasure;
And the song grows glad
or sweet or sad,
As we choose to fashion
the measure.

Ella Wheeler Wilcox

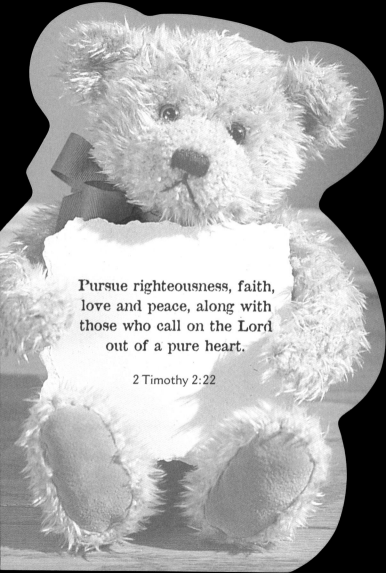

Pursue righteousness, faith,
love and peace, along with
those who call on the Lord
out of a pure heart.

2 Timothy 2:22

Love is the key to the
universe which unlocks
all doors.

Anonymous

The LORD is gracious and
compassionate,
slow to anger and rich
in love.

Psalm 145:8

May the sun always shine
on your windowpane,
may a rainbow be certain
to follow each rain.
May the hand of a friend
always be near you,
may God fill your heart
with gladness to cheer you.

Irish Blessing

A cheerful friend is like
a sunny day spreading
brightness all around.

John Lubcock

The highest form of
wisdom is kindness.

Linda Berman

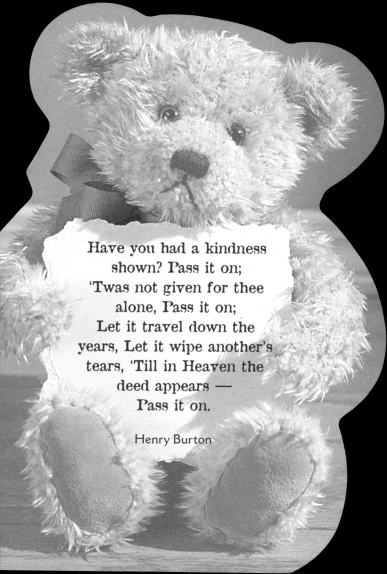

Have you had a kindness
shown? Pass it on;
'Twas not given for thee
alone, Pass it on;
Let it travel down the
years, Let it wipe another's
tears, 'Till in Heaven the
deed appears —
Pass it on.

Henry Burton

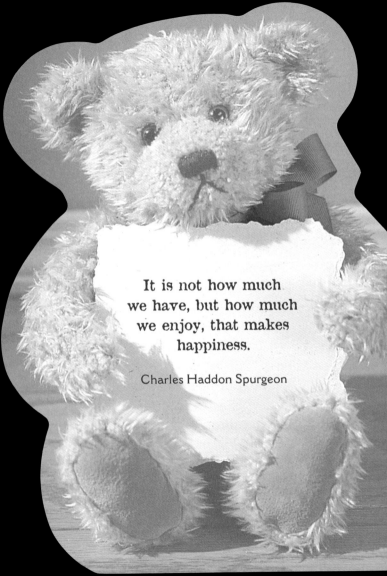

It is not how much
we have, but how much
we enjoy, that makes
happiness.

Charles Haddon Spurgeon

The LORD watches over all who love him.

Psalm 145:20

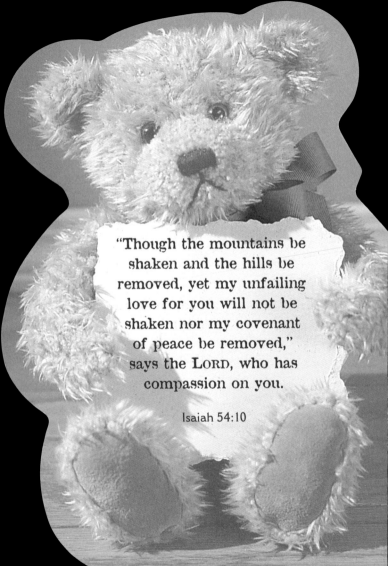

"Though the mountains be
shaken and the hills be
removed, yet my unfailing
love for you will not be
shaken nor my covenant
of peace be removed,"
says the LORD, who has
compassion on you.

Isaiah 54:10

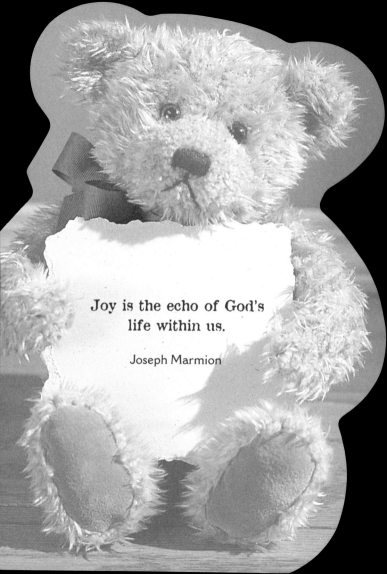

Joy is the echo of God's
life within us.

Joseph Marmion

I delight greatly in the
LORD; my soul rejoices in
my God.

Isaiah 61:10

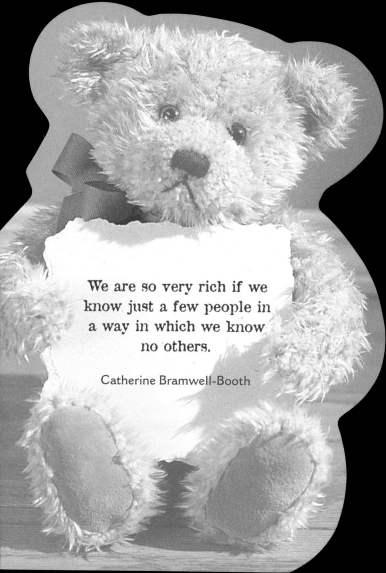

We are so very rich if we
know just a few people in
a way in which we know
no others.

Catherine Bramwell-Booth

Love makes people look
at the bright side of
things. They do see the
bad things, but they
make a great effort to see
the good, so they do see
the good.

Anonymous

Make a rule, and pray God
to help you keep it, never,
if possible, to lie down at
night without being able to
say: "I have made one
human being at least a
little wiser, or a little
happier, or at least a little
better this day."

Charles Kingsley

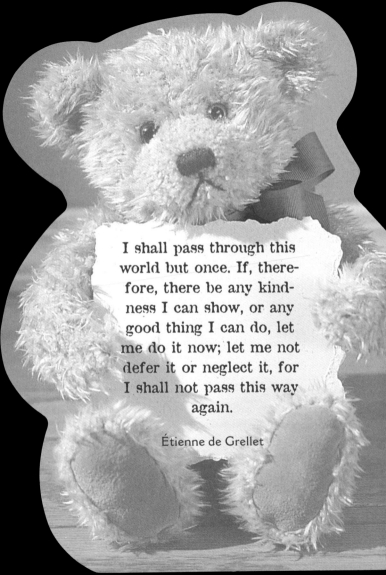

I shall pass through this world but once. If, therefore, there be any kindness I can show, or any good thing I can do, let me do it now; let me not defer it or neglect it, for I shall not pass this way again.

Étienne de Grellet

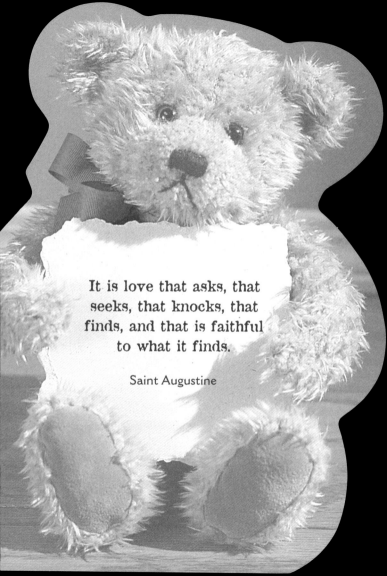

It is love that asks, that seeks, that knocks, that finds, and that is faithful to what it finds.

Saint Augustine

God has made everything
beautiful in its time.

Ecclesiastes 3:11

A true friend is the best possession.

Unknown

The best mirror is an
old friend.

George Herbert

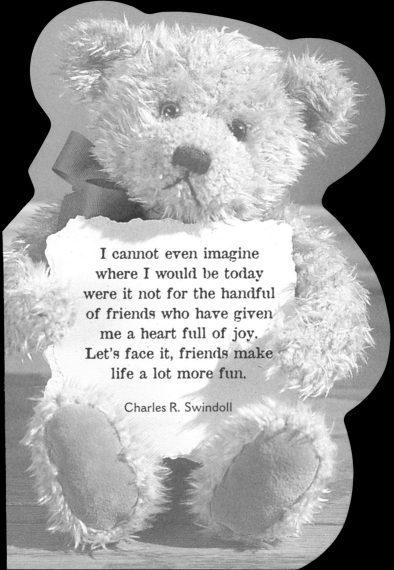

I cannot even imagine
where I would be today
were it not for the handful
of friends who have given
me a heart full of joy.
Let's face it, friends make
life a lot more fun.

Charles R. Swindoll

The heart that loves is
always young.

Anonymous

You have made known to me the path of life, O LORD; you will fill me with joy in your presence, with eternal pleasures at your right hand.

Psalm 16:11

The greatest thing
one can do for his
heavenly Father is to be
kind to some of His
other children.

Henry Drummond

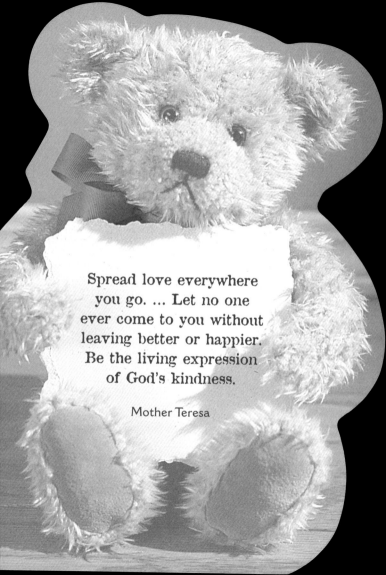

Spread love everywhere
you go. ... Let no one
ever come to you without
leaving better or happier.
Be the living expression
of God's kindness.

Mother Teresa

The heart of him who
truly loves is a paradise
on earth; he has God in
himself, for God is love.

Abbé de Lamennais

Do not be anxious about anything, but in everything, by prayer and petition, with thanksgiving, present your requests to God. And the peace of God, which transcends all understanding, will guard your hearts.

Philippians 4:6–7

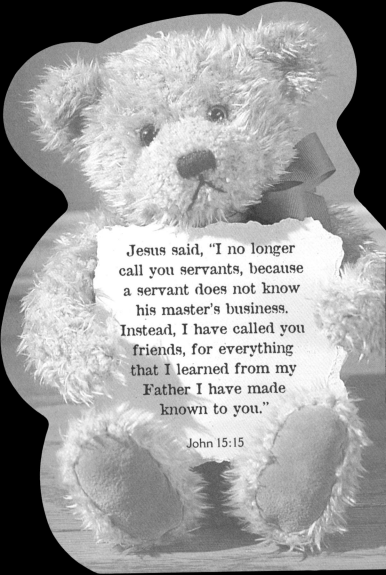

Jesus said, "I no longer call you servants, because a servant does not know his master's business. Instead, I have called you friends, for everything that I learned from my Father I have made known to you."

John 15:15

Human things must be known to be loved; but Divine things must be loved to be known.

Blaise Pascal

God be with you till we
meet again;
By His counsels guide,
uphold you,
With His sheep securely
fold you;
God be with you till we
meet again.

Jeremiah Eames Rankin

Love spends his all, and
still hath store.

Philip James Bailey

A true friend is the greatest of all blessings, and
the one that we take the
least care of all to
acquire.

Françios Duc de La
Rochefoucauld

Praise be to the God and
Father of our Lord Jesus
Christ, who has blessed us
in the heavenly realms
with every spiritual blessing in Christ.

Ephesians 1:3

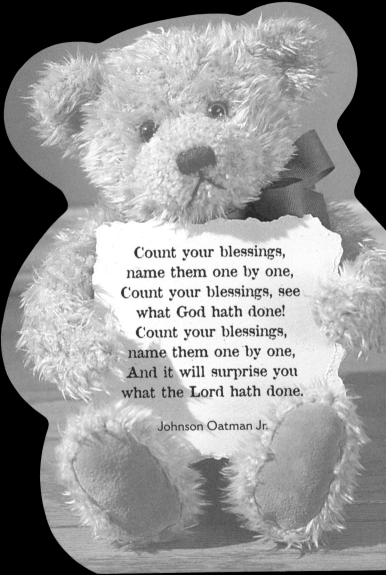

Count your blessings,
name them one by one,
Count your blessings, see
what God hath done!
Count your blessings,
name them one by one,
And it will surprise you
what the Lord hath done.

Johnson Oatman Jr.

Cast all your anxiety
on God because he
cares for you.

1 Peter 5:7

The Lord be with us as
we walk
Along our homeward
road;
In silent thought or
friendly talk
Our hearts be near to
God.

John Ellerton

May the God who gives endurance and encourage-ment give you a spirit of unity among yourselves as you follow Christ Jesus.

Romans 15:5

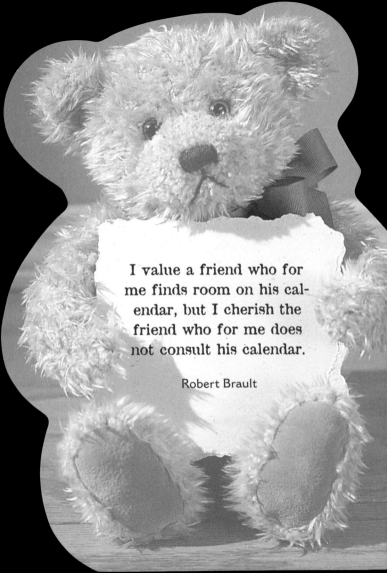

I value a friend who for me finds room on his calendar, but I cherish the friend who for me does not consult his calendar.

Robert Brault

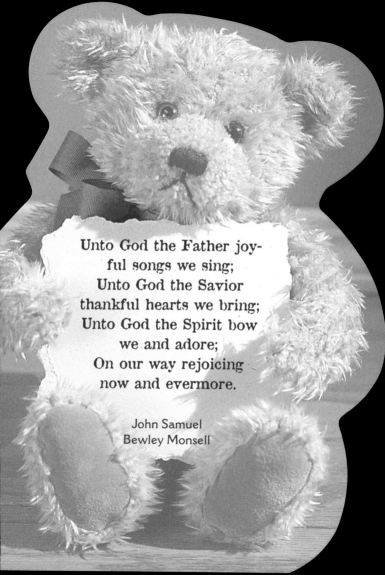

Unto God the Father joy-
ful songs we sing;
Unto God the Savior
thankful hearts we bring;
Unto God the Spirit bow
we and adore;
On our way rejoicing
now and evermore.

John Samuel
Bewley Monsell

True friendship ought never to conceal what it thinks.

Saint Jerome

Never shall I forget the
time which I spent with
you ... continue to be my
friend as you shall always
find me yours.

Unknown

In the morning, prayer
is the key that opens to
us the treasures of God's
mercies and blessings; in
the evening, it is the key
that shuts us up under
His protection and
safeguard.

Anonymous

A friend loves at all times.

Proverbs 17:17

The guardian angels of life
sometimes fly so high as
to be beyond our sight, but
they are always looking
down upon us.

Jean Paul Richter

I can do everything through Christ who gives me strength.

Philippians 4:13

My God will meet all your needs according to his glorious riches in Christ Jesus.

Philippians 4:19

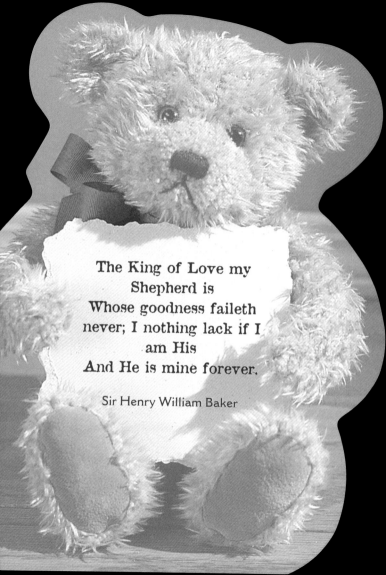

The King of Love my
Shepherd is
Whose goodness faileth
never; I nothing lack if I
am His
And He is mine forever.

Sir Henry William Baker

Faith is the wire that con-
nects you to grace, and
over which grace comes
streaming from God.

Anonymous

Sweet souls around us
watch us still,
Press nearer to our side;
Into our thoughts, into
our prayers, With gentle
helpings glide.

Harriet Beecher Stowe

Perfume and incense
bring joy to the heart,
and the pleasantness of
one's friend springs from
his earnest counsel.

Proverbs 27:9

Surely goodness and love
will follow me
all the days of my life,
and I will dwell in
the house of the LORD
forever.

Psalm 23:6

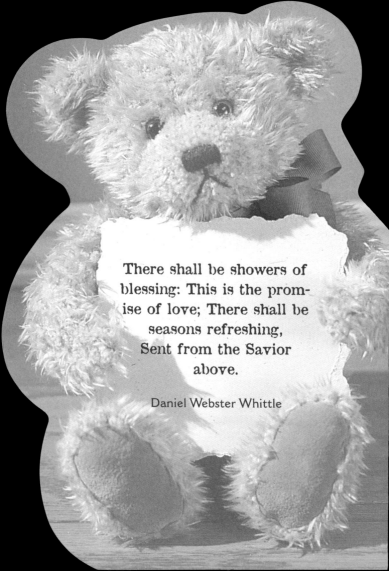

There shall be showers of blessing: This is the promise of love; There shall be seasons refreshing, Sent from the Savior above.

Daniel Webster Whittle

The wings of prayer carry
high and far.

Anonymous

Love is the only service
that power cannot
command and money
cannot buy.

Anonymous

Real friends are those
who, when you feel you've
made a fool of yourself,
don't feel you've done a
permanent job.

Unknown

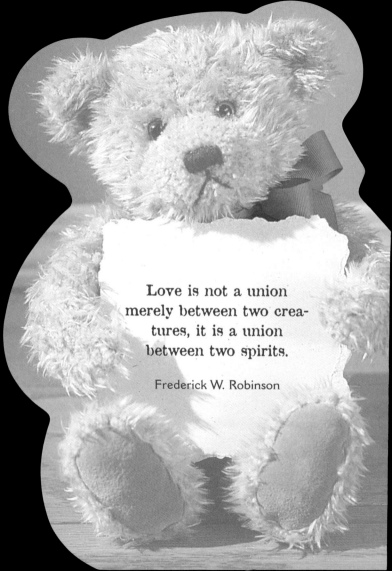

Love is not a union
merely between two crea-
tures, it is a union
between two spirits.

Frederick W. Robinson

Just as you received Christ Jesus as Lord, continue to live in him, rooted and built up in him, strengthened in the faith as you were taught, and overflowing with thankfulness.

Colossians 2:6–7

Your worst days are never
so bad that you are
beyond the reach of God's
grace. And your best days
are never so good that
you are beyond the need
of God's grace.

Jerry Bridges

A coincidence is when God
performs a miracle, and
He chooses to remain
anonymous.

Unknown

Praise God, from Whom
all blessings flow;
Praise Him, all creatures
here below;
Praise Him above, ye
heavenly host;
Praise Father, Son, and
Holy Ghost.

Thomas Ken

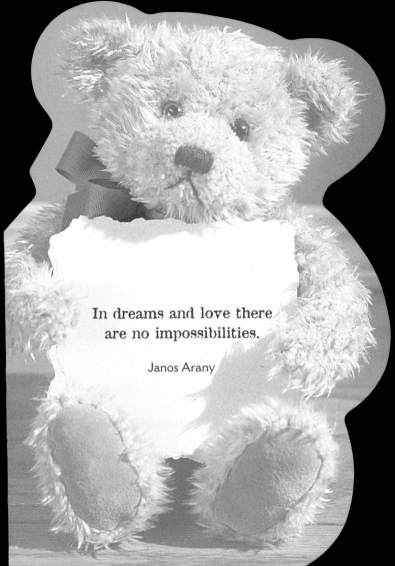

In dreams and love there
are no impossibilities.

Janos Arany

Love shows in so many ways, those who love will always see it, It speaks in so many voices, those who love will always hear it, Love is ... for so many reasons, those who love will never ask why.

Unknown

You make flowers of my
hours. Today was a
bouquet.

Peter McWilliams

Two are better than
one, because they have
a good return for
their work: If one
falls down, his friend
can help him up.

Ecclesiastes 4:9 –10

To love someone is to
see a miracle invisible
to others.

Francois Mauriac

The world is round and
the place which may seem
like the end may also be
only the beginning.

Unknown

From the rising of the sun
to the place where it sets,
the name of the LORD is
to be praised.

Psalm 113:3

The LORD makes my feet
like the feet of a deer;
he enables me to stand
on the heights.

2 Samuel 22:34

To the world you might
be one person, but to one
person you might just
be the world.

Unknown

The ingredients of a
great friendship:
A warm hug to greet
A kind word to cheer
A sweet treat to eat
A few tears to share
Laughter the dark
clouds to part
God's love to warm
each heart

MCD

God saw a tear, and wiped
it away with a smile from
a friend.

Unknown

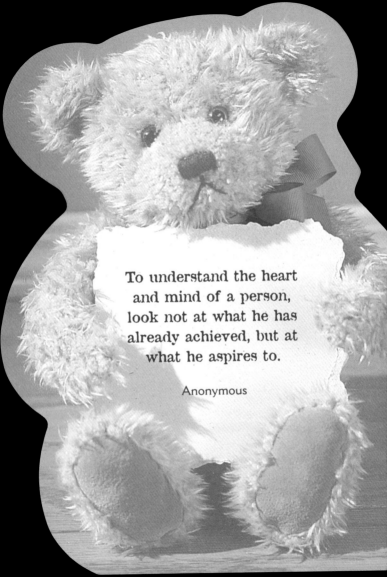

To understand the heart
and mind of a person,
look not at what he has
already achieved, but at
what he aspires to.

Anonymous

There is a time for everything, and a season for
every activity under
heaven.

Ecclesiastes 3:1

Love's a thing that's
never out of season.

Barry Cornwall

Life is a flower of which
love is the honey.

Victor Hugo

How sweet, how heavenly
is the sight,
When those who love
the Lord
In one another's
peace delight,
And so fulfill His Word!

Joseph Swain

To accomplish great things
we must not only act, but
also dream; not only plan,
but also believe.

Unknown

To God who is able to do
immeasurably more than
all we ask or imagine,
according to his power
that is at work within us,
to him be glory in the
church and in Christ Jesus
throughout all genera-
tions, for ever and ever!

Ephesians 3:20 –21

Love is not only something
you feel, it is something
you do.

David Wilkerson

Dear children, let us not
love with words or tongue
but with actions and
in truth.

1 John 3:18

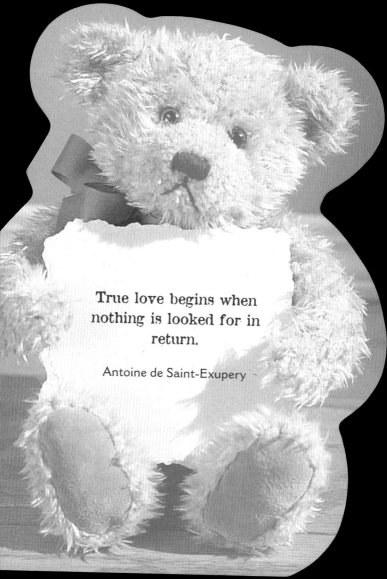

True love begins when nothing is looked for in return.

Antoine de Saint-Exupery

Love is too strong a word
to say too early, but it has
too beautiful a meaning
to say it too late.

Kurt Spiteri Cornish

Each day I'll do a golden
deed, By helping those
who are in need, My life
on earth is but a span,
And so I'll do the
best I can.

William M. Golden

The LORD bless you
and keep you;
the LORD make his face
shine upon you
and be gracious to you;
the LORD turn his face
toward you
and give you peace.

Numbers 6:24 –26